Calvary
a Lenten Rosary Reflection

Sr. Patricia M. McCormack, IHM

Liguori

Imprimi Potest:
Stephen T. Rehrauer, CSsR, Provincial
Denver Province, The Redemptorists

Published by Liguori Publications
Liguori, Missouri 63057

To order, visit Liguori.org or call 800-325-9521.

Copyright © 2015 Liguori Publications

All rights reserved. No part of this publication may be reproduced, stored in a retrieval system, or transmitted in any form or by any means—electronic, mechanical, photocopy, recording, or any other—except for brief quotations in printed reviews, without the prior written permission of Liguori Publications.

p ISBN 978-0-7648-2618-4
e ISBN 978-0-7648-7051-4

Quotations from Vatican documents are used with permission. *Copyright Libreria Editrice Vaticana.*

The wording of the prayers on pages 29–31 are used with permission and taken from usccb.org, the website of the United States Conference of Catholic Bishops. EWTN.com is the source of the concluding prayer on page 32.

Liguori Publications, a nonprofit corporation, is an apostolate of the Redemptorists. To learn more about the Redemptorists, visit Redemptorists.com.

Printed in the United States of America
19 18 17 16 15 / 5 4 3 2 1
First Edition

Through his apostolic letter, *On the Most Holy Rosary* (2002), Pope St. John Paul II enriched devotion to the rosary. Through this encyclical he offered us four gifts:

1. He added the Mysteries of Light.
2. He suggested a creative style of praying the Hail Mary beads, a style that aids contemplation of Jesus through Mary.
3. He called us to adapt the rosary to different spiritual traditions.
4. He invited continued experimentation aimed at leading the praying person to imitate the core values that are contained in the mysteries.

This Stations of the Cross rosary blends three prayer forms:

- The fifteen stations provide a visual focus and body movement.
- The Hail Mary bead incorporates a "Jesus clause" that gives a detail of the mystery. Pope St. John Paul II explained that "the center of gravity in the Hail Mary" is the name of Jesus. And so adding a "who clause" to the name of Jesus becomes a contemplative exercise. For instance:

Hail Mary, full of grace, the Lord is with you; blessed are you among women, and blessed is the fruit of your womb, Jesus, who was given the help of Simon because the soldiers feared he would die along the way and escape the torture of crucifixion.

- Each bead adapts the Ignatian tradition of naming a desired grace that is particular to the mystery. This grace or fruit applies to our own living of the Gospel value that we are contemplating. For example:

Increase my faith in God's ability to make all things work together for good, even the impure motivations of others.

Walk the Stations of the Cross with your rosary in hand, using the "who clauses" and prayers provided in this pamphlet. Or use the visual aid of the station to prompt your own Jesus meditations. Accompany Jesus through his suffering. Be there for him.

During some prayer occasions, situate your own experiences of rash judgment, undeserved punishment, betrayal, abandonment, torments, falls, mistreatment, cruelty, vulnerability, scapegoat occasions, and emotional or physical deaths within Jesus' passion. Join your suffering to the suffering of Jesus. Take on the mind of Christ. Bury your hurts in his tomb. Pray for the grace of forgiveness.

At other prayer times, stand in the sandals of Pilate, the scourging soldiers, the crucifixion soldiers, the religious leaders, a person in the mob, or the tomb guards. Acknowledge the occasions when you have filled such roles.

Then humbly thank Jesus for the occasions of grace when you behaved like his Mother Mary, Veronica, Simon, the "good thief," the sorrowful women, John, Mary Magdalene, Joseph of Arimathea, Nicodemus, or the soldier who proclaimed, "Truly this was the Son of God."

Seek the grace to recognize the ways you are (or have been) each of these characters. Strive to put on the mind of Jesus and Mary. Ask them to develop within you whatever would make you a more dependable companion on the road to Calvary.

How to Pray the Stations of the Cross Rosary

The traditional fourteen Stations of the Cross are the focus of this rosary. The stations are divided into five themes to form the five decades. Hail Mary meditations will lead you to contemplate Jesus' passion by using the "who clausal" style of prayer recommended by Pope St. John Paul II. Each bead ends by asking for a specific grace (written in italics), a practical way to imitate Jesus in your daily living. These petitions for grace are merely suggestions. Feel free to replace them with petitions of your own choosing. Also, pages 29–31 feature the words of these prayers: the Sign of the Cross; Apostles' Creed; Our Father; Glory Be; Fatima; Hail, Holy Queen; and Hail Mary, followed by the traditional closing prayer of the rosary.

1. On the crucifix, pray the Sign of the Cross.

2. On the introductory beads, pray the:
   (A) Apostles' Creed, **(B)** three Hail Marys (for an increase in faith, hope, and charity), and a **(C)** Glory Be.

3. On the large bead that starts each decade, pause to read the meditative thought that introduces the decade. When you are ready to begin the decade, pray the Our Father.

4. Focus on the image of the Station of the Cross. On each small bead pray:
   - Hail Mary, full of grace, the Lord is with you; blessed are you among women, and blessed is the fruit of your womb, Jesus, who…
   - the "who clause" that refers to Jesus
   - pray the petition for grace.

5. On the tenth bead of the decade, add:
   - "Holy Mary, Mother of God, pray for us sinners now and at the hour of our death. Amen."
   - the Glory Be.
   - the Fatima Prayer, if desired.

6. Announce the next decade and repeat steps three through five.

First Decade

Be Nondefensive in the Face of Mistreatment

Jesus was subjected to betrayal, perjury, unjust sentencing to capital punishment, scourging, and mockery. He was abused physically and emotionally. Regardless, Jesus did not accept the identity of victim. He looked instead to his Father for definition. He was the beloved Son in whom the Father was well pleased. His self worth and dignity came directly from his Father. So does ours! When we know who we are and whose we are, there is no need for defense or explanation.

Pray the Our Father

Station 1: Jesus Is Condemned

- Hail Mary, full of grace, the Lord is with you; blessed are you among women, and blessed is the fruit of your womb, Jesus, who was taken to Pilate by the religious leaders and accused of treason since they did not have the power to put him to death. *Teach me to act justly.*

- Hail Mary, full of grace, the Lord is with you; blessed are you among women, and blessed is the fruit of your womb, Jesus, who remained silent throughout Pilate's interrogation. *Develop in me a nondefensive attitude.*
- Hail Mary, full of grace, the Lord is with you; blessed are you among women, and blessed is the fruit of your womb, Jesus, who was mocked, scourged, tormented, spat upon, and less valued than Barabbas. *Root my self-image in the opinion God the Father holds of me.*
- Hail Mary, full of grace, the Lord is with you; blessed are you among women, and blessed is the fruit of your womb, Jesus, of whom Pilate said, "I am innocent of the blood of this just man." *Establish within me unity in speech and action.*

Station 2: Jesus Takes His Cross

- Hail Mary, full of grace, the Lord is with you; blessed are you among women, and blessed is the fruit of your womb, Jesus, who accepted the cross and began the journey through the narrow streets to Golgotha. *Teach me how to grow through the crosses in my life.*

- Hail Mary, full of grace, the Lord is with you; blessed are you among women, and blessed is the fruit of your womb, Jesus, who carried his cross through the streets while merchants continued business as usual, oblivious to, or unconcerned for, his unjust suffering. *Move me away from focusing on "me, myself, and I."*

- Hail Mary, full of grace, the Lord is with you; blessed are you among women, and blessed is the fruit of your womb, Jesus, whose weakened physical condition continued to deteriorate, making the cross unmanageable. *Give me the humility to resign myself to personal inadequacy.*

Station 3: Jesus Falls for the First Time

- Hail Mary, full of grace, the Lord is with you; blessed are you among women, and blessed is the fruit of your womb, Jesus, who, despite his desire to embrace the cross, fell under the weight of it. *Tutor my heart to value effort more than achievement.*

- Hail Mary, full of grace, the Lord is with you; blessed are you among women, and blessed is the fruit of your womb, Jesus, who accepted his human inadequacy and renewed his effort to embrace the cross. *Strengthen my will in the face of challenge and temptation.*

- Hail Mary, full of grace, the Lord is with you; blessed are you among women, and blessed is the fruit of your womb, Jesus, who modeled that the spirit can be strong though the body may be weak. *Enkindle in me a desire for God that surpasses the limitations of body, mind, and spirit.*

Holy Mary, Mother of God, pray for us sinners now and at the hour of our death, Amen.

Pray the Glory Be

Optional: Pray the Fatima Prayer

Second Decade

Accept Human Support

Jesus and Mary met along the path of pain. Neither was adequate to relieve the suffering of the other but both were willing to bear their suffering in trust. Motivated by expediency, soldiers forced Simon to assist Jesus. Through their tears and cries, women protested the inhumane cruelty inflicted on Jesus. For one woman, empathy overshadowed fear of reprisal and she dared to wipe Jesus' bloodied face. Compassion comes in many sizes. It blesses the one who receives and it stretches the one who gives.

Pray the Our Father

Station 4: Jesus Meets His Mother

- Hail Mary, full of grace, the Lord is with you; blessed are you among women, and blessed is the fruit of your womb, Jesus, whose unjust suffering pierced your soul. *Develop within me empathy and compassion for others who suffer.*

- Hail Mary, full of grace, the Lord is with you; blessed are you among women, and blessed is the fruit of your womb, Jesus, whose glance met yours and communicated purpose. *Teach me to be present to the needs of others.*

- Hail Mary, full of grace, the Lord is with you; blessed are you among women, and blessed is the fruit of your womb, Jesus, in whose passion you shared. *Give me the grace to embrace my own suffering without complaint.*

Station 5: Simon the Cyrenian Helps Jesus

- Hail Mary, full of grace, the Lord is with you; blessed are you among women, and blessed is the fruit of your womb, Jesus, whose physical stamina was mortally impaired. *Give me patient endurance when I encounter health problems or feelings of diminishment.*

- Hail Mary, full of grace, the Lord is with you; blessed are you among women, and blessed is the fruit of your womb, Jesus, who was given the help of Simon because the soldiers feared he would die along the way and escape the torture of crucifixion. *Increase my faith in God's Providence to make all things work together for my good—even the impure motivations of others.*

- Hail Mary, full of grace, the Lord is with you; blessed are you among women, and blessed is the fruit of your womb, Jesus, who accepted Simon's help and shared the burden of the cross. *Move me to allow others to help me.*

- Hail Mary, full of grace, the Lord is with you; blessed are you among women, and blessed is the fruit of your womb, Jesus, who invites me to be a Simon for others who struggle under the weight of a cross. *Sensitize me to the burdens that another person carries.*

Station 6: Veronica Helps Jesus

- Hail Mary, full of grace, the Lord is with you; blessed are you among women, and blessed is the fruit of your womb, Jesus, who was refreshed and affirmed by the sensitivity of Veronica. *Move me today to serve as a Veronica to someone.*

- Hail Mary, full of grace, the Lord is with you; blessed are you among women, and blessed is the fruit of your womb, Jesus, who calls me to grow in compassion and service. *Stretch my heart to imitate you.*

- Hail Mary, full of grace, the Lord is with you; blessed are you among women, and blessed is the fruit of your womb, Jesus, who challenges me to be a Veronica to others and do what I can to alleviate suffering instead of being paralyzed by what I cannot do. *Hone in me the humility to place both my strengths and my limitations at the service of the Gospel.*

Holy Mary, Mother of God, pray for us sinners now and at the hour of our death, Amen.

Pray the Glory Be

Optional: Pray the Fatima Prayer

Third Decade

Choose to Love Regardless of Circumstances

Soldiers took sport in inflicting pain on Jesus. Some in the crowd taunted with derision. Even with the help of Simon, Jesus fell several times. His beaten body and thorn-crowned head throbbed with pain. And still Jesus responded with compassion to women in the crowd. In all circumstances Jesus focused on his mission: to do the will of God, to be Love. Jesus demonstrated that love is a choice. Love transcends circumstances of pain, suffering, and human brokenness.

Pray the Our Father

Station 7: Jesus Falls a Second Time
- Hail Mary, full of grace, the Lord is with you; blessed are you among women, and blessed is the fruit of your womb, Jesus, who was abused physically and emotionally each time he fell. *Make me respectful of the limitations of others and gentle with myself when I fall.*

- Hail Mary, full of grace, the Lord is with you; blessed are you among women, and blessed is the fruit of your womb, Jesus, who fell even though Simon was helping to carry the cross. *Open me to recognize the Simons in my life and to be a Simon to others.*

- Hail Mary, full of grace, the Lord is with you; blessed are you among women, and blessed is the fruit of your womb, Jesus, whose second fall teaches me to focus on effort rather than on outcome. *Develop in me a purity of intention in all that I do.*

- Hail Mary, full of grace, the Lord is with you; blessed are you among women, and blessed is the fruit of your womb, Jesus, whose fall teaches me to persevere through struggle. *Tutor my heart through my falls and failings.*

Station 8: Jesus Consoles the Women

- Hail Mary, full of grace, the Lord is with you; blessed are you among women, and blessed is the fruit of your womb, Jesus, who showed compassion for the weeping women in the midst of his own suffering. *Grow in me the grace to receive the service of others graciously.*

- Hail Mary, full of grace, the Lord is with you; blessed are you among women, and blessed is the fruit of your womb, Jesus, who focused on the needs of others in the midst of his own pain. *Pattern me to reach beyond myself to respond to others.*

- Hail Mary, full of grace, the Lord is with you; blessed are you among women, and blessed is the fruit of your womb, Jesus, who challenges me to rise above self-centeredness and become other-centered. *Empower me to be more concerned with giving than receiving.*

Station 9: Jesus Falls a Third Time

- Hail Mary, full of grace, the Lord is with you; blessed are you among women, and blessed is the fruit of your womb, Jesus, whose will remained resolute despite the conditions of his body. *Focus me on God's will when I experience my own emptiness.*

- Hail Mary, full of grace, the Lord is with you; blessed are you among women, and blessed is the fruit of your womb, Jesus, who fell and was beaten along the way while onlookers jeered. *Strengthen me to be attentive to the Father's goals for me regardless of the reactions of others.*

- Hail Mary, full of grace, the Lord is with you; blessed are you among women, and blessed is the fruit of your womb, Jesus, who illustrated that the will of the soul can rise above human suffering. *Draw me to you when I experience my limitations.*

Holy Mary, Mother of God, pray for us sinners now and at the hour of our death, Amen.

Pray the Glory Be

Optional: Pray the Fatima Prayer

Fourth Decade

Overcome Evil with Love

Torn flesh matted in blood and the dust of the earth clung to the garments the soldiers ripped off Jesus. The stripping reopened wounds that had already clotted. Crucifixion was capital punishment that intended indignity, humiliation, and total vulnerability. Hours of pain and agony preceded death. Such torture combined with heat, hunger, and the contempt of spectators could quite easily bring out the worst of any person. And yet on Calvary Jesus demonstrated consideration of others, forgiveness, reconciliation, dependence on God, fidelity to his mission, and active acceptance of his suffering and death. Jesus replaced the human instinct to react in kind with the supernatural choice to respond in love.

Pray the Our Father

Station 10: Jesus Is Stripped

- Hail Mary, full of grace, the Lord is with you; blessed are you among women, and blessed is the fruit of your womb, Jesus, who was stripped of his garments which reopened the wounds of his scourging. *Renew within me the grace of forgiveness when old wounds open in my soul.*

- Hail Mary, full of grace, the Lord is with you; blessed are you among women, and blessed is the fruit of your womb, Jesus, who stood naked, exposed, and vulnerable, but without shame. *Develop in me a self-possession that has no need of defensiveness, power, or prestige.*

- Hail Mary, full of grace, the Lord is with you; blessed are you among women, and blessed is the fruit of your womb, Jesus, who entered the world in poverty and left it possessing nothing but the love of God. *Cultivate within me a love so strong that God is my enough.*

Station 11: Jesus Is Crucified

- Hail Mary, full of grace, the Lord is with you; blessed are you among women, and blessed is the fruit of your womb, Jesus, who was nailed to the cross without the anesthetizing of pain. *Draw me to imitate your response to suffering.*

- Hail Mary, full of grace, the Lord is with you; blessed are you among women, and blessed is the fruit of your womb, Jesus, who was mounted between two thieves who were both guilty of their crimes. *Teach me your humility to make no distinction between myself and others.*

- Hail Mary, full of grace, the Lord is with you; blessed are you among women, and blessed is the fruit of your womb, Jesus, who promised salvation to the repentant thief. *Make me an instrument of Good News to all people.*

- Hail Mary, full of grace, the Lord is with you; blessed are you among women, and blessed is the fruit of your womb, Jesus, who was taunted and ridiculed while hanging on the cross in agony. *Grace me to practice the Beatitude virtue of meekness when I am hurt by others.*

Station 12: Jesus Dies

- Hail Mary, full of grace, the Lord is with you; blessed are you among women, and blessed is the fruit of your womb, Jesus, whose cross became a pulpit, the most powerful of his ministry. *Let the manner of my dying give glory to you.*

- Hail Mary, full of grace, the Lord is with you; blessed are you among women, and blessed is the fruit of your womb, Jesus, who practiced prayerful union with his father and unconditional obedience. *Tutor my heart to live every day the virtues I want others to see in me, especially at the time of my death.*

- Hail Mary, full of grace, the Lord is with you; blessed are you among women, and blessed is the fruit of your womb, Jesus, who participated freely in his crucifixion and death. *Grace me to be an active agent in my transformation process.*

Holy Mary, Mother of God, pray for us sinners now and at the hour of our death, Amen.

Pray the Glory Be

Optional: Pray the Fatima Prayer

Fifth Decade

Rely on Divine Providence

Jesus was born in the stable of an innkeeper and he was buried in the tomb of a Jewish council member. In Bethlehem, Mary laid him in a manger; in Jerusalem others took his broken body from her arms and laid him in a tomb. At significant life moments, Jesus and Mary were dependent upon the goodwill of others. Always they were dependent upon the providential care of God. From crib to cross, from tomb to triumph, they trusted that God would provide.

Pray the Our Father

Station 13: Jesus is Taken Down from the Cross

- Hail Mary, full of grace, the Lord is with you; blessed are you among women, and blessed is the fruit of your womb, Jesus, from whose lanced side flowed blood and water. *Teach me how to separate needs from wants and offer both to you.*

- Hail Mary, full of grace, the Lord is with you; blessed are you among women, and blessed is the fruit of your womb, Jesus, whose bruised, lifeless body you cradled in your arms. *Empower me to be a comforting presence to those who grieve the death of a loved one.*

- Hail Mary, full of grace, the Lord is with you; blessed are you among women, and blessed is the fruit of your womb, Jesus, in whose sacrifice you participated as Co-Redemptrix. *Make me a catalyst of plentiful redemption to all I meet.*

Station 14: Jesus Is Buried

- Hail Mary, full of grace, the Lord is with you; blessed are you among women, and blessed is the fruit of your womb, Jesus, whose body was prepared for burial by Joseph of Arimathea and Nicodemus and then laid in a nearby tomb. *Empower me to prepare myself for death, releasing hurts, resentments, anger, and the desire for retaliation.*

- Hail Mary, full of grace, the Lord is with you; blessed are you among women, and blessed is the fruit of your womb, Jesus, whose tomb had been hewn from a formation of rock and was enclosed by a huge stone. *Let your tabernacle serve as the tomb for whatever needs to die within me.*

- Hail Mary, full of grace, the Lord is with you; blessed are you among women, and blessed is the fruit of your womb, Jesus whose tomb was sealed and guarded by order of the chief priests and the Pharisees. *Set a guard at the door of my heart and a seal on my lips when life-blocking thoughts stir within me.*

- Hail Mary, full of grace, the Lord is with you; blessed are you among women, and blessed is the fruit of your womb, Jesus, who challenges me to let die and to bury anything that blocks the life that Jesus came to bring. *Deliver me from anything within myself that blocks your presence or frustrates your will.*

Station 15: Resurrection

- Hail Mary, full of grace, the Lord is with you; blessed are you among women, and blessed is the fruit of your womb, Jesus, who fulfilled the Scripture by rising from the dead on the third day. *Deepen within me confidence that you will always fulfill your promises to me.*

- Hail Mary, full of grace, the Lord is with you; blessed are you among women, and blessed is the fruit of your womb, Jesus, who appeared to Mary Magdalene, the disciples of Emmaus, the apostles, and surely to you! *Move me to recognize the moments when Jesus visits me today.*

- Hail Mary, full of grace, the Lord is with you; blessed are you among women, and blessed is the fruit of your womb, Jesus, who teaches me that I cannot experience the joy of Easter without first entering into the painful loss of Good Friday. *Instill in me a creative hope during times of sorrow.*

Holy Mary, Mother of God, pray for us sinners now and at the hour of our death, Amen.

Pray the Glory Be

Optional: Pray the Fatima Prayer

As you conclude, spend time in silence, meditating on these mysteries of the rosary and the Stations of the Cross. When you are ready:

Pray the Hail Holy Queen

End with the Sign of the Cross

Prayers

Sign of the Cross

In the name of the Father, the Son, and the Holy Spirit. Amen.

The Apostles' Creed

I believe in God, the Father almighty, Creator of heaven and earth, and in Jesus Christ, his only Son, our Lord, who was conceived by the Holy Spirit, born of the Virgin Mary, suffered under Pontius Pilate, was crucified, died and was buried; he descended into hell; on the third day he rose again from the dead; he ascended into heaven, and is seated at the right hand of God the Father almighty; from there he will come to judge the living and the dead. I believe in the Holy Spirit, the holy catholic Church, the communion of saints, the forgiveness of sins, the resurrection of the body, and life everlasting. Amen.

Our Father

Our Father, who art in heaven, hallowed be thy name; thy kingdom come; thy will be done on earth as it is in heaven. Give us this day our daily bread; and forgive us our trespasses as we forgive those who trespass against us; and lead us not into temptation, but deliver us from evil. Amen.

Hail Mary

Hail Mary, full of grace, the Lord is with you; blessed are you among women, and blessed is the fruit of your womb, Jesus.

Holy Mary, Mother of God, pray for us sinners now and at the hour of our death. Amen.

The Glory Be (the Doxology)

Glory be to the Father, the Son, and the Holy Spirit; as it was in the beginning, is now, and ever shall be, world without end. Amen.

Fatima Prayer

O my Jesus, forgive us our sins, save us from the fires of hell, lead all souls to Heaven, especially those who have most need of your mercy.

Hail, Holy Queen

Hail, holy Queen, mother of mercy, our life, our sweetness, and our hope. To you we cry, poor banished children of Eve; to you we send up our sighs, mourning and weeping in this valley of tears. Turn, then, most gracious advocate, your eyes of mercy toward us; and after this, our exile, show unto us the blessed fruit of your womb, Jesus. O clement, O loving, O sweet Virgin Mary.

V. Pray for us, O Holy Mother of God.
R. That we may be made worthy of the promises of Christ.

Let us Pray: *O God, whose only begotten Son by his life, death, and resurrection has purchased for us the rewards of eternal salvation, grant, we beseech you, that while meditating upon these mysteries of the holy rosary of the Blessed Virgin Mary that we may imitate both what they contain and obtain what they promise, through the same Christ, our Lord. Amen.*